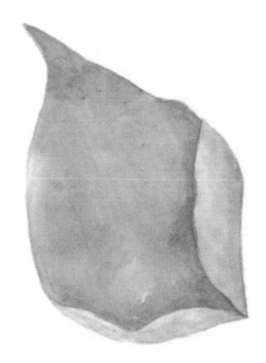

This Dream Journal
Belongs To

_____

My Dream Ticket Journal

Set out in 3 Stages

1. My Dreams
2. My Beliefs
3. Manifestations

Copyright ©
Mary McCallion Dempsey

Introduction

I am excited for you ☺

You have literally downloaded
your Dream Ticket **into** you.
You now give yourself full
permission to **GO for it** .

No more holding back.
No more hiding your gift,
your dream.

Now is your time. You already listened to your Dream calling – now
you are ready for the next magical step ....to create it and ground it
into being.

I am excited for you and for the world, because our dreams are not
just for ourselves. They may come through us but our dreams call us to
not only make our life and world better, but through us, to make The
World a better place.

Your Dream is so connected to who you are, and your purpose for
being. This is where its magic lies. It plays with you and calls you out of
the doldrums of life and into the Dance.

Your Dream is your Soul's calling card. It wants to be birthed into being.
The exciting, though scary thing is… it has chosen YOU as its way of
coming into the world.

That's great news – but like I say, it's also scary. Why would it be scary?
Well if it weren't scary then the dream and landing that dream would
be an instant thing. Like having a magic wand.

So why aren't our dreams like magic wands?
It's the hidden things we bump into that prevents the magic from happening here and now.

There's a journey ...a process that we and our dream must embark on. You know this, and that's why you are drawn to this dream ticket workbook & journal.

You see. as much as
we create our dreams our dreams create us.

So that's what this workbook is about. It is your guide to manifesting your dream. It will guide your steps so that you don't get lost or fall into any potholes or fall by the wayside as many dreams do. Following the steps in this workbook and journaling along the way will grow your dream. It will easily move it from a tiny frightened concept in your head. It will embody it into reality. You will give it shape. You will give it life. You will breathe it into being.

This is who we are, this is who you are at the core of your being. You are the creator of your world and you take your prompts from the Master Creator.

How will it help?
- ✓ It will help you navigate your journey from where you are now to where you want to be.

- ✓ It will help expose those little hidden pockets of fear and self-doubt that are keeping you stuck and preventing you moving forward.

- ✓ It will begin to unvail the clear path you seek.

When we have our dream, our vision of how we want things to be, we get excited and eager to get going. But we find that we are not making the progress we want.

Why? Because we come up against so many frustrating invisible blocks.

They are invisible to us because we come up against ourselves.
- We come up against our judgements our attitudes our fears.
- We doubt ourselves in ways we never imagined.
- The main thing we come up against is our lack of Belief in our selves.

One of the biggest blocks that can remain hidden is our *belief that we are not good enough* to manifest such a magnificent dream or life. This is what leads us into self-sabotage – blocking our progress and preventing ourselves from having what we actually want.

The bonus of uncovering your self-sabotaging gremlins is that once you shine a light on them – magic happens. They become transformed into your little helpers and guide you to your next steps in achieving and grounding your dream.

It might be that Job you've always wanted. It goes something like this.:

Now the opportunity has presented itself and you've been motivated enough and excited enough to apply for the job. You've got the interview – fantastic! You prepare – but sometimes we over prepare. We don't trust ourselves to do well at the interview.

Problem is that this is what we bring in with us to the interview and guess what ….it becomes true. It becomes a self-fulfilling prophecy. We don't get the job. This is due to this little gremlin hidden away in our subconscious mind telling you "You know you're not up to this job" …" you know this is way beyond you". So you're unconscious protector kicks in and prevents you getting the job. All with the best of intentions to protect you from you're unconscious fears of actually getting the job of your dreams.

In doing the inner work that you will be guided to do here in your workbook and journal, you will uncover those, unconscious fears, little gremlins. They will soon get to know that from now on you are in charge!!

So here we go! I hope your ready! Ready for take off !!!

Stage 1

Step 1 Where are you? This is a major step ...because each subsequent step DEPENDS on accessing this one as accurately as you can.

So, in relation to your Dream this calls for you to tune in ...sit quiet ...Breathe ....and gather up the information. Use these spaces below to gather your thoughts and beliefs about where you are now.

You wouldn't believe how many people try to skip this one. I know I do. It's called impatience. We're all in a hurry to get there. But the journey is all part of the fun too. It's an important one because as I said, all other steps depend on this foundation.

Just picture setting out on a journey to New York, booking your ticket believing your are in Washington when in fact you are in Ireland!! You wouldn't even get off the ground ☺

Can you feel how much pressure you would create if you start from a false place? We need to know where our feet are standing at the point of take off. That will help launch you on your journey much more directly and save you a lot of pain and frustration on the journey.

Let My Dream Manifest !!!
This workbook Journal will
help bring you into alignment
with your Dream Vibration.
This is the magic of creation.

♡

You are The
Magic

You are here!

Stage 1

Dreams

Know where are you starting
from!

"Until one is committed, there is hesitancy, the chance to draw back. Concerning all acts of initiative (and creation), there is one elementary truth, the ignorance of which kills countless ideas and splendid plans: that the moment one definitely commits oneself, then Providence moves too. All sorts of things occur to help one that would never otherwise have occurred. A whole stream of events issues from the decision, raising in one's favour all manner of unforeseen incidents and meetings and material assistance, which no man could have dreamed would have come his way. Whatever you can do, or dream you can do, begin it. Boldness has genius, power, and magic in it. Begin it now."

— **W.H. Murray**

# My Dream Life...

_____

_____

_____

_____

_____

_____

_____

_____

_____

_____

_____

_____

NOTES

DREAM PLANNER

Dream Steps

NOTES:

♡ Intuitive Downloads

_____

_____

_____

_____

_____

_____

_____

_____

_____

_____

_____

_____

_____

Dream Doodles

Action

Daily To Dos

- [ ]
- [ ]
- [ ]
- [ ]
- [ ]

Calls to Make

_____

_____

_____

_____

_____

_____

Appointments

_____

_____

_____

_____

_____

_____

Notes / Thoughts / Ideas / Gratitude

_____

_____

_____

_____

_____

You are Here

Baggage Accessment

My Blocks...

_____

_____

_____

_____

_____

_____

_____

_____

_____

_____

_____

_____

_____

NOTES

Intuitive Downloads

Dream Doodles

22

Action

Daily To Dos

☐ ☐ ☐
☐ ☐ ☐
☐ ☐ ☐
☐ ☐ ☐
☐ ☐ ☐

Calls to Make

_____

_____

_____

_____

_____

_____

Appointments

_____

_____

_____

_____

_____

_____

Notes / Thoughts / Ideas / Gratitude

_____

_____

_____

_____

♡ My Beliefs...

NOTES

♡ Intuitive Downloads

Dream Doodles

 I Deserve....

NOTES

NOTES

Intuitive Downloads

_____

_____

_____

_____

_____

_____

_____

_____

_____

_____

_____

_____

Dream Doodles

Action

Daily To Dos

☐ ☐ ☐

☐ ☐ ☐

☐ ☐ ☐

☐ ☐ ☐

☐ ☐ ☐

Calls to Make | Appointments

_____ _____

_____ _____

_____ _____

_____ _____

_____ _____

Notes / Thoughts / Ideas / Gratitude

_____

_____

_____

_____

_____

My Doubts & Fears?

NOTES

♡ Intuitive Downloads

Dream Doodles

Stage 2

Beliefs

I believe…..

I create

I decide…

I Choose…

I receive with gratitude…

I give with Joy

I am Abundant…in health…& wealth….

©mary@angelwhispers.ie

Beliefs I let go of....

NOTES

Behaviours I now let go of....

NOTES

♡ Intuitive Downloads

Dream Doodles   m

42

Action

Daily To Dos

☐   ☐   ☐

☐   ☐   ☐

☐   ☐   ☐

☐   ☐   ☐

☐   ☐   ☐

Calls to Make   Appointments

Notes / Thoughts / Ideas / Gratitude

I let go of Old Stressors....

NOTES

Attitudes to let go of ....

My New Attitudes ....

Dream Doodles   m

NOTES

Intuitive Downloads

Dream Doodles   m

Action

Daily To Dos

- [ ]   [ ]   [ ]
- [ ]   [ ]   [ ]
- [ ]   [ ]   [ ]
- [ ]   [ ]   [ ]
- [ ]   [ ]   [ ]

Calls to Make

Appointments

Notes / Thoughts / Ideas / Gratitude

Self Sabotaging Patterns....

Habits to let go of.....

....

....

♡ Emotional

....

....

♡ Thoughts

....

....

♡ Behaviours

....

....

♡ People

....

....

♡♡ Places

....

....

....

I Accept
All The Love That
Flows to Me
Today & Always

Self Sabotaging Patterns....

Emotional Habits I to let go of.....

_____

_____

_____

_____

_____

_____

_____

_____

_____

_____

_____

_____

_____

Self Sabotaging Patterns....

♡ Thoughts to let go of.....

NOTES

NOTES

Self Sabotaging Patterns....

People who drain my energy....

_____

_____

_____

_____

_____

_____

_____

_____

_____

_____

_____

_____

_____

_____

NOTES

Self Sabotaging Patterns....

Places that drain my energy....

_____

_____

_____

_____

_____

_____

_____

_____

_____

_____

_____

_____

_____

NOTES

Procastinating Habits

Time

♡My New Time Bank

Dream Doodles   m

NOTES

Action

Daily To Dos

- [ ]   [ ]   [ ]
- [ ]   [ ]   [ ]
- [ ]   [ ]   [ ]
- [ ]   [ ]   [ ]
- [ ]   [ ]   [ ]

Calls to Make   Appointments

_____   _____

_____   _____

_____   _____

_____   _____

_____   _____

Notes / Thoughts / Ideas / Gratitude

_____

_____

_____

_____

Procastinating Habits

Money

· · · ·

Dream Doodles

NOTES

Self Care Time

Create Time For..... Me.....Family & Friends.

You are Here

Ready For Take Off

♡

My Magic Manifesting Map

Create You Inner Satna

The Essential Steps:

Managing Mindset

Self Care
Needs

Ask & Receive

Time

Managing Mindset

My Guiding Beliefs....

NOTES

Managing Mindset

♡ I Choose....

NOTES

Managing Mindset

♡ I Deserve

_____

_____

_____

_____

_____

_____

_____

_____

_____

_____

_____

_____

_____

NOTES

Managing Mindset

Decisive Decisions

NOTES

Managing Mindset

My Guiding Emotions

Emotions & Feelings I want more of in my life

NOTES

Managing Mindset
Raise My Vibe ♡

What gives me energy ....

NOTES

Managing Mindset

My Confident Mindset

Dream Doodles   m

NOTES

Action

Daily To Dos

- [ ]   [ ]   [ ]
- [ ]   [ ]   [ ]
- [ ]   [ ]   [ ]
- [ ]   [ ]   [ ]
- [ ]   [ ]   [ ]

Calls to Make	Appointments
_____	_____
_____	_____
_____	_____
_____	_____
_____	_____

Notes / Thoughts / Ideas / Gratitude

_____

_____

_____

_____

Angelwhispers
✦ Create The Life You'll Love To Live

99

You must have a dream to unlock the magic in you ...

MARY @ANGELWHISPERS.IE

www.angelwhispers.ie ♥

87

Managing Mindset

My Dream Aligned Identity

NOTES

Intuitive Downloads

Dream Doodles   m

Action

Daily To Dos

- [ ]   [ ]   [ ]
- [ ]   [ ]   [ ]
- [ ]   [ ]   [ ]
- [ ]   [ ]   [ ]
- [ ]   [ ]   [ ]

Calls to Make

Appointments

_____
_____
_____
_____
_____

Notes / Thoughts / Ideas / Gratitude

Ask & You Shall Receive

Needs?

_____

What help do I need? Who?

_____

Finance

_____

Time

_____

_____

_____

_____

_____

_____

_____

_____

_____

Self Care Time

Create Time For..... Me..... Family & Friends.

My Needs....

Personal....

My Needs....

♡

Professional .....

_____

_____

_____

_____

_____

_____

_____

_____

_____

_____

_____

_____

_____

_____

_____

NOTES

I Need.....

Finances

NOTES

Things I can do

NOTES

Action

Daily To Dos

- [ ]   [ ]   [ ]
- [ ]   [ ]   [ ]
- [ ]   [ ]   [ ]
- [ ]   [ ]   [ ]
- [ ]   [ ]   [ ]

Calls to Make

_____

_____

_____

_____

_____

Appointments

_____

_____

_____

_____

_____

Notes / Thoughts / Ideas / Gratitude

_____

_____

_____

_____

NOTES

Things I Need Help with....
(outsource - time savers stress savers)

NOTES

Dreams are our inner maps
to total freedom
of our soul!

Charlie Ward FB

My New Self Care Habits

Create Time For......

Relaxation

Meditation

Mind expansion

Exercise

NOTES

Intuitive Downloads

Dream Doodles   m

Action

Daily To Dos

- [ ]
- [ ]
- [ ]
- [ ]
- [ ]
- [ ]
- [ ]
- [ ]
- [ ]
- [ ]
- [ ]
- [ ]
- [ ]
- [ ]
- [ ]

Calls to Make

Appointments

Notes / Thoughts / Ideas / Gratitude

NOTES

My Dream Made Easy
Productive Habits

No Excuses

My Dream Made Easy
Productive Habits

My New Self Care Habits   ♡

NOTES

I am Grateful for ....

NOTES

Intuitive Downloads

Dream Doodles   m

Action

Daily To Dos

- [ ]   [ ]   [ ]
- [ ]   [ ]   [ ]
- [ ]   [ ]   [ ]
- [ ]   [ ]   [ ]
- [ ]   [ ]   [ ]

Calls to Make   ## Appointments

NOTES

Well Done
You Have Landed!!!

♡

Imagination is evidence of the Divine
William Blake

Believe   Create   Divine
Awareness
Start
Choose
Clear
Decide
Just be   Do it
Love
Joy   Blessed   Grateful
Healthy
Abundant
Wise
Patience
Reap your reward.
Let it be easy....guided   Higher Mind. Choose You
Conscious Mind   Dream plant Subconscious
Mind.
Creator
Imagination
Connected
Giving

♡

Planning Resources

My WEEKLY PLANNER

DATE:_____

Inspirations:

M T W T F S S

Daily Goals:

1 _____
2 _____
3 _____
4 _____
5 _____

TO DO LIST:

☐ _____
☐ _____
☐ _____
☐ _____
☐ _____
☐ _____
☐ _____
☐ _____
☐ _____
☐ _____
☐ _____
☐ _____

Dream Dodles

NOTES

My **Monthly** Dream Plan

My Motivation for the Month

Top 3 Intentions for the Month | Dates to Remember

Work

Health

Spiritual

Relationships

Notes

NOTES

My WEEKLY PLANNER

DATE: _____

Inspirations: ♡

M T W T F S S

Daily GoalS:

1 _____
2 _____
3 _____
4 _____
5 _____

TO DO LIST:

☐ _____
☐ _____
☐ _____
☐ _____
☐ _____
☐ _____
☐ _____
☐ _____
☐ _____
☐ _____
☐ _____
☐ _____

Dream Dodles

NOTES

My **Monthly** Dream Plan

_____
_____
_____
_____

Top 3 Intentions for the Month

Dates to Remember

Work
_____
_____
_____

Health
_____
_____

Spiritual

Notes
_____
_____

Relationships
_____
_____
_____

NOTES

My WEEKLY PLANNER

DATE: _____

M T W T F S S

Daily GoalS:

1 _____
2 _____
3 _____
4 _____
5 _____

TO DO LIST:

☐ _____
☐ _____
☐ _____
☐ _____
☐ _____
☐ _____
☐ _____
☐ _____
☐ _____
☐ _____
☐ _____
☐ _____

Inspirations: ♡

Dream Dodles

NOTES

My **Monthly** Dream Plan

_____
_____
_____
_____

Top 3 Intentions for the Month	Dates to Remember

Work

_____
_____
_____

Health

_____
_____
_____

Spiritual

_____
_____
_____

Relationships

_____
_____
_____

Notes

_____
_____
_____
_____
_____
_____
_____

NOTES

My WEEKLY PLANNER

DATE: _____

Inspirations:

M T W T F S S

Daily Goals:

1 _____
2 _____
3 _____
4 _____
5 _____

TO DO LIST:

- ☐ _____
- ☐ _____
- ☐ _____
- ☐ _____
- ☐ _____
- ☐ _____
- ☐ _____
- ☐ _____
- ☐ _____
- ☐ _____
- ☐ _____
- ☐ _____

Dream Dodles

NOTES

My **Monthly** Dream Plan

My Motivation for the Month

_____

_____

_____

_____

Top 3 Intentions for the Month	Dates to Remember

Work

_____

_____

_____

Health

_____

_____

_____

Spiritual

_____

_____

_____

Relationships

_____

_____

_____

Notes

_____

_____

_____

_____

_____

_____

_____

NOTES

My WEEKLY PLANNER

DATE: _____

Inspirations: ♡

M T W T F S S

Daily GoalS:

1 _____
2 _____
3 _____
4 _____
5 _____

TO DO LIST:

☐ _____
☐ _____
☐ _____
☐ _____
☐ _____
☐ _____
☐ _____
☐ _____
☐ _____
☐ _____
☐ _____
☐ _____

Dream Dodles

NOTES

My **Monthly** Dream Plan

My Motivation for the Month

_____

_____

_____

_____

Top 3 Intentions for the Month	Dates to Remember

Work

_____

_____

_____

Health

_____

_____

_____

Spiritual

_____

_____

_____

Relationships

_____

_____

_____

Notes

_____

_____

_____

_____

_____

_____

_____

182

NOTES

♡

What are you
BELIEVING....about YOU....about
your world....whatever it
is....that's what you are
CREATING. Awareness is the
starting point to clearing out
and choosing what you want in
your life....and then planting
the belief that matches what you
desire. Add patience & faith.
Reap your reward. ♡ make it
easy....be guided by you're
Higher Mind. Choose with your
Conscious Mind and plant in
your Subconscious Mind.

My WEEKLY PLANNER

DATE: _____

Inspirations: ♡

M T W T F S S

Daily GoalS:

1 _____
2 _____
3 _____
4 _____
5 _____

TO DO LIST:

☐ _____
☐ _____
☐ _____
☐ _____
☐ _____
☐ _____
☐ _____
☐ _____
☐ _____
☐ _____
☐ _____
☐ _____

Dream Dodles

124

NOTES

My **Monthly** Dream Plan

My Motivation for the Month

_____

_____

_____

_____

Top 3 Intentions for the Month

Dates to Remember

Work

_____

_____

Health

_____

_____

Spiritual

Notes

_____

_____

_____

Relationships

_____

_____

_____

_____

NOTES

For more
Magical Manifesting inspiration,
skills and resources
You will find them
@

www.angelwhispers.ie

mary@angelwhispers.ie

Books I want to Read

Classes I want to Take

2020 at a glance

January
S	M	T	W	T	F	S
			1	2	3	4
5	6	7	8	9	10	11
12	13	14	15	16	17	18
19	20	21	22	23	24	25
26	27	28	29	30	31	

February
S	M	T	W	T	F	S
						1
2	3	4	5	6	7	8
9	10	11	12	13	14	15
16	17	18	19	20	21	22
23	24	25	26	27	28	29

March
S	M	T	W	T	F	S
1	2	3	4	5	6	7
8	9	10	11	12	13	14
15	16	17	18	19	20	21
22	23	24	25	26	27	28
29	30	31				

April
S	M	T	W	T	F	S
			1	2	3	4
5	6	7	8	9	10	11
12	13	14	15	16	17	18
19	20	21	22	23	24	25
26	27	28	29	30		

May
S	M	T	W	T	F	S
					1	2
3	4	5	6	7	8	9
10	11	12	13	14	15	16
17	18	19	20	21	22	23
24	25	26	27	28	29	30
31						

June
S	M	T	W	T	F	S
	1	2	3	4	5	6
7	8	9	10	11	12	13
14	15	16	17	18	19	20
21	22	23	24	25	26	27
28	29	30				

July
S	M	T	W	T	F	S
			1	2	3	4
5	6	7	8	9	10	11
12	13	14	15	16	17	18
19	20	21	22	23	24	25
26	27	28	29	30	31	

August
S	M	T	W	T	F	S
						1
2	3	4	5	6	7	8
9	10	11	12	13	14	15
16	17	18	19	20	21	22
23	24	25	26	27	28	29
30	31					

September
S	M	T	W	T	F	S
		1	2	3	4	5
6	7	8	9	10	11	12
13	14	15	16	17	18	19
20	21	22	23	24	25	26
27	28	29	30			

October
S	M	T	W	T	F	S
				1	2	3
4	5	6	7	8	9	10
11	12	13	14	15	16	17
18	19	20	21	22	23	24
25	26	27	28	29	30	31

November
S	M	T	W	T	F	S
1	2	3	4	5	6	7
8	9	10	11	12	13	14
15	16	17	18	19	20	21
22	23	24	25	26	27	28
29	30					

December
S	M	T	W	T	F	S
		1	2	3	4	5
6	7	8	9	10	11	12
13	14	15	16	17	18	19
20	21	22	23	24	25	26
27	28	29	30	31		

Printed in Poland
by Amazon Fulfillment
Poland Sp. z o.o., Wrocław

58058319R00085